CW00823331

Healthy JUNK 2

by **SHARNY & JULIUS**

*50 more healthy versions of
your favourite junk foods!*

www.sharnyandjulius.com
email:sharnyandjulius@
sharnyandjulius.com

Copyright © the Kieser Publishing Trust
First published by Kieser Publishing Trust
in May 2014
The moral rights of the authors have been
asserted. The stories, suggestions and
opinions of the authors are their personal
views only, and they are simply that, just
stories, not historical accounts. The strategies
and steps outlined in the book may not work
for everyone. Due diligence and thorough
research is always recommended.

All rights reserved. This book may not be
reproduced in whole or in part, stored, posted
on the internet or transmitted in any form
or by any means, electronic, mechanical,
photocopying, recording, or other, without
written permission from the Authors and
publisher of the book.

Cover Photography: sharnyandjulius

Typesetting and Design: sharnyandjulius

ISBN: 978-0-9923613-8-9

HEALTHY JUNK2

MORE HEALTHY VERSIONS OF YOUR FAVOURITE JUNK FOODS!

50 MORE GUILT-FREE DELICIOUS RECIPES

sugar free
wheat free
grain free
nut free
dairy free
additive free
preservative free
guilt free
paleo friendly

ohhh so tasty!

SHARNY ⑤ JULIUS
www.sharnyandjulius.com

Thank you Again

When we first released Healthy Junk, we didn't anticipate how big it would become. In less than a year, it is as if it has a life of it's own.

And we owe that to you.

Without you, the first book would have been a failure. We hope that this book lives up to your expectations, and like all our kids, has it's own life - one of great service to others.

Thankyou again, from the bottom of our hearts. We love you and we will continue creating useful recipes until we run out, or you tell us to stop. The world is getting healthier. Last year, we couldn't say that, but this year we can feel it.

Health and wellness are a priority, and you are the pioneer. Stay healthy, stay hungry, stay focussed. What feels like paddling against a current will become paddling with the current. The tide is turning. Thanks to you, humanity has a new focus.

Stay ahead, we need you as a shining beacon of possibility. We'll be right behind you, making sure everybody else catches up, and nobody gets left behind.

All our love

SHARNY ☒ JULIUS

Menu
in alphabetical order, because when it comes to junk food, well, there is no 'right time'...)

Apple Tea Cake

Ingredients:

Cake
½ cup coconut flour
½ cup tapioca starch
1 cup water
1 tbsp baking soda
¼ tsp Himalayan sea salt
½ tsp ground cinnamon
½ tsp vanilla extract
¼ cup coconut oil, melted
½ cup coconut nectar
3 large eggs
150g diced red apples
1 tbsp lemon juice (juice of about ½ a lemon)
1 tsp apple cider vinegar

Cinnamon swirl
1 tbsp cinnamon
1½ tbsp coconut oil, melted
2 tbsp coconut nectar

Glaze
2 tbsp coconut oil
2 tbsp freshly puréed apple
2 tbsp coconut nectar
4 tbsp coconut cream

This recipe has 3 parts, the cake, the pattern on top (we call it the cinnamon swirl) and the glaze.

How to make:

Preheat oven to 180°C (350°F).

Oil your round cake tin all sides with coconut oil.

Mix the apples and lemon juice together and leave in a bowl.

Mix the coconut flour, tapioca, baking soda, cinnamon, and salt in a blender (if you don't have a blender use a medium sized bowl).

Add water, coconut oil, eggs, coconut nectar, vanilla and ACV.

Fold in the apple mixture (don't blend it).

Put ingredients into the cake tin and spread evenly.

Mix the cinnamon swirl ingredients in a small bowl, then drizzle around the cake.

Use a toothpick to spread the mixture around and make patterns.

Bake for 30 minutes, or until toothpick comes out clean.

Cool on a wire rack, then use a knife to loosen the sides from the pan.

Flip the cake out gently and put on a plate.

Mix together all of your glaze ingredients in a blender and drizzle over tea cake to make it all shiny like…

S and J tip – Keep well in fridge for 2 days.

Banana Milkshake

Ingredients:

1 ½ cups of milk (coconut milk or almond milk)

2 bananas (frozen or fresh)

2 tbsp of desiccated coconut

2 fresh dates (seed removed)

1 cup of ice (only if bananas aren't frozen)

How to make:

Add all ingredients to the blender and blend for 2 minutes.

S and J tip – If you use fresh ripe bananas that aren't frozen add a cup of ice.

Beef Stock

Ingredients:

2 kg beef bones (with lots of marrow), including some knuckle bones if possible, cut to expose the center marrow, and include at least a couple veal bones if you can, for their gelatin

500g of extra stewing beef (optional)

1 chopped onion

2 chopped carrots

2 celery stalks

1 chopped leek

1 clove of fresh garlic finely chopped

2 tbsp of coconut vinegar (or apple cider vinegar)

1L of water

Himalayan sea salt

Pepper

1 - 2 bay leaves

Parsley and other fresh herbs

How to make:

Put all your ingredients (except 1 litre of water) with some coconut oil in a pan in the oven for 45 minutes on 200°C until meat goes brown.

Tip all ingredients into a large pot and add 1 litre of water.

Bring to a boil.

Turn it to low heat and simmer with a lid for 5 hours.

Strain the liquid into a container and store on the fridge.

If there is any fat on the top of the stock after a few hours in the fridge, scrape it off and put it in the bin.

S and J tips – Ask your butcher to cut large tubular beef bones in half so that you can get to the nutritious bone marrow. (Make sure this is good quality organic grass fed beef.)

Berry Pullapart

Ingredients:

¾ cup coconut flour

½ cup tapioca starch

¾ cup coconut sugar

¼ tsp Himalayan sea salt

1 tbsp baking powder

¼ tsp guar gum

½ cup coconut oil

3 large eggs

3 tbsp apple sauce

Filling: ½ cup of jam (see our recipe on page 64)

Optional White Glaze:

1 tbsp powdered Erythritol mixed with 1 tbsp water until it becomes a paste

How to make:

Preheat oven to 180°C.

Mix the coconut flour, tapioca, sugar, salt, baking powder and guar gum in a blender or bowl.

Add the coconut oil, eggs and apple sauce.

Put the dough between two sheets of baking paper and roll out into a rectangle about an inch thick.

Remove top sheet of baking paper and spread the jam filling over the surface of the dough.

Roll the dough up like a carpet.

Use the baking paper to help with rolling so it don't stick to your fingers.

Place a sheet of baking paper in square baking tin. Wipe a little oil onto the bottom of the tin and sprinkle a little coconut sugar into the tin too.

Sprinkle some tapioca starch on the roll so it stays together better while cutting.

Slice each roll 2 inches wide and lay into the tin beside each other (they'll end up sticking together to make one big yummy delicious slab of happiness).

Cover the baking tin with aluminium foil and bake for 50 minutes.

Remove the foil and bake for another 10 minutes.

Cool before devouring.

Caramel Chews

Ingredients:

¼ cup melted chocolate (see HealthyJUNK1)

½ cup coconut nectar

2 tbsp coconut oil

3 tbsp tapioca starch

1 tsp pure vanilla extract

2 cup coconut sugar (blended to a fine powder)

(these taste like columbines)

How to make:

Mix all of the ingredients in a blender or mixing bowl.

Pour your ingredients into a container lined with baking paper.

Put in the freezer until caramel goes hard.

Cut and store in freezer.

S and J tip – Once cut you can dip them in HJ chocolate, put in the freezer to make chocolate fantails.

Caramel Tarts

Ingredients:

Crust
½ cup coconut oil

½ cup coconut nectar

3 cups shredded coconut

2 tbsp raw cacao powder

Caramel filling
10 dates

Pinch of Himalayan sea salt

⅓ cup coconut cream

How to make:

Crust:
Preheat the oven to 180°C.

Melt and mix the coconut oil and coconut nectar in a small saucepan on low heat. Add coconut and cacao and combine well.

Press mixture into the base and up the sides of a standard sized quiche dish or pie tin.

Bake the crust for 30 minutes.

Remove from the oven and let cool and harden.

Caramel:
Process dates and salt until they form a paste and then slowly add the coconut cream.

Fill the crust with caramel.

Store in fridge.

Carbonara

Ingredients:

Sauce
1 cup coconut cream
1 tbsp coconut oil
4 tsp tapioca starch
Pinch of Himalayan sea salt
Pinch of pepper
2 cloves garlic chopped

Filling
500g of chicken breast
1 onion diced
1 cup chopped bacon

Noodles
3 sweet potato, spiralled (we use a Spirooli machine, or you can grate them)
2 - 3 tbsp coconut oil for cooking the sweet potatoes

How to make:

Dice and fry the chicken breast with onions until cooked through.

Set aside.

In a saucepan combine the cream, oil, starch, salt, pepper, garlic.

Heat until thickened, stirring the whole time.

Set aside.

Cook sweet potato noodles in saucepan (medium heat) until soft.

Mix noodles, sauce and filling together in a big bowl and serve.

Ingredients:

Cake
2 medium carrots (grated)

1 cup tapioca starch

½ cup coconut flour

1 tbsp baking powder

½ tsp ground cinnamon

½ cup coconut sugar

¾ cup coconut oil

½ cup coconut nectar

3 eggs

1 tsp vanilla essence

½ cup roasted pepitas

Icing
180g creamed goats cheese (same consistency as cream cheese)

¼ cup coconut nectar

¼ tsp pure vanilla essence

Carrot Cake

How to make:

Cake:
Preheat oven to 180°C.

Grease a small round cake tin lightly with some coconut oil and line with non stick baking paper.

Mix all ingredients except carrots and pepitas in a large bowl or blender.

Now gently stir in grated carrot and pepitas.

Scoop the mixture into the cake tray. Filling it to the top as your cake will not rise much.

Bake for 35 – 40 minutes.

Set aside to cool for about 10 minutes.

Turn out onto a wire rack to cool completely.

Icing:
Place the goats 'cream' cheese, coconut nectar and vanilla in a bowl. Use a wooden spoon to mix until well combined.

Spread the icing over the cooled cake.

Chicken and Leek Pie

Ingredients:

Filling
500g cooked diced chicken
1 tbsp coconut oil
1 tsp tapioca starch
1 onion sliced
½ cup leek sliced
1 carrot diced (optional)
1 cup of fresh corn kernels
from the cob (optional)
1 cup chicken stock
180g coconut milk
1 tsp thyme chopped
1 tsp english mustard
1 clove garlic finely chopped

Pastry
2 tsp whole psyllium husks
⅛ tsp guar gum
⅓ cup of warm water.
1 ¾ cup of golden linseeds
blended (flaxmeal)
½ cup tapioca starch
¼ tsp Himalayan sea salt
½ tbsp baking powder
1 clove garlic finely chopped
(optional for more flavour)
1 tbsp paprika powder
(optional for more flavour)
May need extra water

24

How to make:

Filling:
Cook on the stove on medium heat for around 30 minutes when it should a
thicken.

Pastry:
Preheat oven to 180°C.

In a small cup or bowl combine the psyllium, guar gum and ⅓ cup of water. Mi
and set aside for a few minutes so that it can thicken.

Mix the flaxmeal, tapioca, salt and baking powder in a blender.

Add the psyllium mix and blend on high.

If your dough is crumbly, add a little bit more water (1 tsp at a time) until it start
to hold together.

Place your mixture between two sheets of baking paper and roll out very thin.
Too thick and it will end up way too hard.

Spread your dough out in a pie tray (Family tray or minis) and add your filling.
Put a pastry lid on each pie (or one big ol' one on that family pie).

Bake for 25 minutes on 180°C.

S and J tip – Feel free to add whatever spices and seasoning to your pastry a
you like to add different flavour. This pastry has a very strong flavour, so keep i
really thin (thinner than the photo) so it doesn't overpower the filling.

Psyllium husks look a little like rice, except empty. You'll see what I mean when
you get them. LOL.

Chicken and Tomato Bake

Ingredients:

4 sliced chicken breast pieces or 8 - 10 chicken legs

1 cup pureed fresh tomatoes

2 tbsp of 'no salt' tomato paste

1 diced onion

3 cloves of garlic finely chopped

Juice of 1 lemon

1 tsp mustard

1 tsp paprika

2 tbsp apple cider vinegar

1 tsp coconut aminos

1 tsp Himalayan sea salt

Pepper to taste (about ¼ tsp)

1 quinoa or cauliflower rice (optional)

How to make:

Preheat oven to 180°C.

Lay chicken and onion into baking dish ready for oven.

Mix other ingredients together and pour over chicken.

Cover with aluminum foil and bake for 1 hour.

Removed cover and cook for a further 10 - 15 minutes.

Serve with freshly cooked quinoa (make sure you soak quinoa if you can for a few hours and then rinse well).

S and J tip - Use cauliflower rice instead of quinoa if you like (**see HealthyJUNK1**).

Chicken Stock

Ingredients:

1 chopped onion

2 chopped carrots

1 chopped leek

1 clove of fresh garlic finely chopped

1 whole chicken or chicken pieces (make sure this is good quality organic/grass fed)

1 tsp coconut oil

1L of water

1 - 2 bay leaves

Pinch of Himalayan sea salt

Pepper

Spring parsley (optional)

How to make:

Add all the ingredients to a pot and boil on stovetop. Make sure your water covers everything in pot. (May need to break up chicken so water covers it).

Then turn it to low to medium heat and simmer with a lid for 2 - 3 hours.

Pull your chicken out and use it in another chicken recipe. Maybe the chicken and leek pie.

Strain the liquid into a container and store on the fridge.

If there is any fat on the top of the stock after a few hours in the fridge, just scrape it off and put it in the bin.

Choc Banana Bites

Ingredients:

2 - 4 bananas sliced

HealthyJUNK1 'Peanut butter'

HealthyJUNK1 Chocolate OR

HealthJUNK2 Raw Chocolate fudge

How to make:

Line a container (or 2) with baking paper.

Peel and slice bananas into about 1cm wide circles.

Lay half of the slices out on baking paper.

Put a tsp of 'HJ Peanut butter' on banana circles.

Add the other banana circles to the top.

Dip each banana bite into chocolate and put back in container.

Cover container with a lid.

Freeze for a few hours or overnight.

Best kept in the freezer.

Chocolate Rolo

Ingredients:

Make HealthyJUNK1 chocolate and leave as a liquid

10 fresh dates (seeds removed)

½ cup water

How to make:

Blend dates and water until smooth and caramel consistency.

Half fill chocolate mould with your liquid chocolate.

Add a tsp or so of caramel.

Fill the rest with your liquid chocolate.

Freeze for at least 2 hours (or overnight).

S and J tip - You can removed the skin of the dates. We have a high-speed blender and it blends fine without removing skin.

Chocolate Bar

Ingredients:

Base layer
2 cups blended sunflower seeds
3 ½ tbsp coconut oil
⅓ cup coconut sugar
⅛ tsp Himalayan sea salt
¼ tbsp baking powder
1 tsp vanilla extract

Caramel layer
¾ cup coconut oil.
1 ¼ cups coconut sugar (blended until fine)
¼ cup coconut nectar
180ml coconut cream
1 tsp pure vanilla extract
½ tsp Himalayan sea salt

Chocolate covering
HealthyJUNK1 Chocolate before you freeze it

Like a Twix Bar... mmmmm...

How to make:

Base layer:
Preheat oven to 180°C.
Combine ingredients in a food processor until crumbly. (This can also be done by hand).
Place a piece of baking paper in a 7x7 pan so that it also covers the sides. (This baking paper will be your means of removing the bars when its time to cover them in chocolate).
Press the crumbly base layer into the bottom of the pan evenly.
Bake at 180°C for 18 - 20 minutes.
Remove from oven and allow to cool and harden in the pan.

Caramel layer:
In a sauce pan, combine the oil, sugar, nectar, coconut cream and salt.
Bring to boil, stirring constantly.
Quickly stir in the vanilla.
Take from stove and allow to sit for 2 minutes and then pour on top of your biscuit base.

Set aside and allow to cool for 30 minutes.
Freeze until hard.
Cut into thin bars and dip into your melted HealthyJUNK1 chocolate.
Put back in freezer for an hour for chocolate to go hard.

S and J tip – If you want to make it more like a Mars bar, just use the caramel chews recipe for your caramel layer.

Chocolate Slice

Ingredients:

Slice
120g coconut oil, melted
½ cup tapioca starch
½ cup coconut flour
1 cup coconut sugar
1 cup desiccated coconut
¼ cup raw cacao powder

Icing
2 tbsp raw cacao powder
1 cup coconut sugar blended
1 tbsp coconut milk
1 tbsp coconut oil, melted

How to make:

Preheat oven to 180°C.

Mix all ingredients in a large bowl, stir well.

Pour into an oven tray lined with baking paper.

Bake for 15 - 20 minutes.

Mix all of your icing ingredients together well.

Pull your slice out of the oven and allow to cool a little and go hard (will be soft when it first comes out of oven).

Spread icing over the warm slice. You can also ice it cold ;)

Sprinkle with your favourite healthy treat. Coconut, crushed sunflower seeds (or raw nuts if you don't have a nut allergy).

Let cool before you cut onto squares.

Chocolate Tart

Ingredients:

Crust
²/₃ cup coconut oil

½ cup coconut nectar

3 cups shredded coconut

2 tbsp raw cacao powder

Filling
270ml can coconut cream

100g HealthyJUNK1 chocolate

½ tsp vanilla bean powder

½ cup coconut nectar

How to make the crust:

Preheat the oven to 180°C.

Melt and mix the coconut oil and coconut nectar in a small saucepan on low heat.

Add shredded coconut and cacao and combine well.

Press mixture into the base and up the sides of a standard sized quiche dish or pie tin.

Bake the crust for 30 minutes. Remove from the oven and let cool and harden.

How to make the Chocolate filling:

Heat the coconut cream and vanilla powder in a saucepan until it simmers.

Put coconut cream into in a mixing bowl.

Add melted chocolate and nectar, whisking it through until silky.

Pour into tart shell, filling 1cm from the top.

Place the tart in the fridge until the filling goes hard.

Crackers

Ingredients:

½ cup sunflower seeds

½ cup sesame seeds

¼ cup chia seeds

¼ cup brown linseeds

½ cup golden linseeds
(blended to make flaxmeal)

250ml water

3 cloves garlic

2 tbsp freshly chopped basil

1 tsp Himalayan sea salt

How to make:

Preheat oven to 150°C.

Combine all ingredient in a bowl.

Spread mixture out on a baking tray lined with baking paper.

Make sure it is thin so that your biscuits are crunchy.

Bake for 30 minutes.

Pull from the oven and cut into the shapes you want.

Flip each cracker and cook for another 30 minutes.

Stores in an air tight container for about a week.

Creamy Seafood Pasta

Ingredients:

1kg of green prawns peeled (you can add other seafood)

250 ml coconut cream

1 tbsp coconut oil (for cooking prawns)

½ cup chicken stock (see our recipe on page 28)

2 tbsp coconut oil

4 spring onions chopped

Cherry tomatoes halved (optional)

1 chilli finely chopped (optional if you love spicy food)

¼ cup parsley

3 cloves of garlic (crushed)

4 tsp tapioca starch

Salt and pepper to taste

White sweet potato, zucchini or egg plant (Put through your spirooli machine)

How to make:

Spiral the pasta like we showed you in HealthyJUNK1.

In a saucepan combine the cream, chicken stock, coconut oil, tapioca, salt, pepper, garlic, parsley, chilli and spring onion; heat until thickened, whisking the whole time; set aside.

In a separate pan, cook your green prawns until orange.

Pour sauce over cooked prawns in pan and let simmer.

Add pasta and sliced cherry tomatoes.

Let simmer for another 3 minutes.

Check the taste to see if a little more salt and pepper is needed.

Serve and enjoy!!

S and J tip – In our picture we used Konjac fettuccine, which is very low in calories (available in most supermarkets).

Crumbed Fish

Ingredients:

4 fresh white ocean fish (for this recipe we used big pieces of barramundi)

About ½ cup of coconut oil (for cooking)

2 large eggs

1 cup quinoa flakes

½ cup quinoa flour

1 tsp of finely chopped fresh garlic

1 tsp of Himalayan sea salt

1 tsp pepper

1 tbsp mixed herbs (optional) (we love fresh oregano and basil finely chopped)

How to make:

Slice fish in half long ways (if big pieces).

Beat eggs in bowl.

In separate bowl, mix all the other ingredients.

Soak each piece of fish in egg, then roll in crumb mixture.

Pour coconut oil into pan on stove and let it get really hot.

Make sure you have about 1cm deep pool of oil.

Add pieces of fish to hot oil and cook both sides.

S and J tip - Serve with chips and tomato sauce from HealthyJUNK1.

Custard Filled Doughnuts

Ingredients:

Doughnut
¼ cup of warm water
2 tsp yeast
1 tbsp of coconut sugar
½ cup of coconut flour
¾ cup tapioca starch
1 tsp guar gum
2 tbsp baking powder
2 tsp amaranth flour
½ tsp Himalayan sea salt
1 cup of coconut sugar
5 tbsp coconut oil
3 large eggs
Coconut oil (for frying Doughnuts)

Custard
1 ½ cup coconut milk
2 eggs
¼ cup coconut sugar blended until fine (coconut nectar is an option and will make your custard a lighter colour.)
1 tsp vanilla extract
¼ tsp Himalayan sea salt
3 tbsp tapioca starch

How to make:

Doughnut:

Preheat oven to 180°C.

Mix the warm water, yeast and tbsp of sugar and let sit.
In a blender, mix the rest of your doughnut ingredients.
Pour in the yeast mixture and blend on high for 1 - 2 minutes until it thickens.
Let the mix sit for 1 - 2 minutes while it gets thicker and stickier.

Put the dough onto your bench dusted with a little tapioca so it doesn't stick.
Roll or pat out the dough to be 1 ½ inches thick.
Using a biscuit cutter or a cup, cut into 8 circles. (Dust the biscuit cutter with starch).

Place the doughnuts onto a baking tray lined with baking paper.
Wipe each doughnut with a little water and cover with baking paper.
Cover the tray with a towel.

Turn the oven off, and place the covered tray into the oven.
Leave the doughnuts in the warm oven for 30 minutes to rise.

Slowly heat a layer of coconut oil in a pan.
Fry your doughnuts. (If you heat it too high your doughnuts will not cook fully on the inside.)
Turn the doughnuts so they cook evenly.

Allow to cool on a wire rack.

Dig a hole inside the Doughnut to make room for filling.

Custard:

Pour coconut milk into a saucepan over low heat.

In a mixing bowl, mix eggs, sugar, vanilla, salt, and tapioca.

Pour warmed coconut milk into mixture and stir until well-mixed.

Pour mixture back into saucepan over medium to high heat, and stir fast until thickened.

Let your custard cool and squeeze into your cooled Doughnuts with a piping bag.

Chocolate: (optional)

Make some HJ1 chocolate and dip the top of each Doughnut in chocolate.

S and J tip – You can add 1 tbsp of cacao powder to your custard mix to make your custard chocolate flavoured.

Also, you can use a doughnut shaped cookie cutter to get a hole on the inside, but then you won't be able to get much custard in.

Double Choc Biscuits

Ingredients:

2 cups sunflower seed butter (see HealthyJUNK1)

⅓ cup raw cacao powder

1 tbsp baking powder

¼ tsp Himalayan sea salt

½ cup coconut sugar

1 tbsp vanilla extract

4 ½ tbsp coconut oil

2 tbsp apple sauce

100g of HealthyJUNK1 chocolate chopped into chunks

How to make:

Preheat oven to 180°C.

Cover a large cookie sheet with baking paper to prevent sticking.

Mix (by hand should work as well) all of the ingredients until the dough come together.

Stir in the chocolate pieces last.

Form cookies with your hands into round / flat patties (I made mine 1 inch thic and about 3 inches wide).

Bake for 15 minutes.

Remove from oven and allow to cool before removing from baking sheet.

Double Choc Muffins

Ingredients:

½ cup coconut flour

½ cup melted HealthyJUNK1 chocolate

½ cup coconut oil

6 eggs

½ cup coconut nectar

2 tsp pure vanilla extract

¼ cup full fat coconut milk

½ tsp apple cider vinegar

¼ cup raw cacao powder

1 tbsp baking powder (HJ1 recipe)

½ tsp Himalayan sea salt

1 cup HealthyJUNK1 chocolate chopped into small pieces to stir in at the end

How to make:

Preheat oven to 180°C.

Over low heat, melt the HealthyJUNK1 chocolate in coconut oil (Stirring frequently).

Allow to cool.

Mix eggs, coconut nectar, vanilla, apple cider vinegar, coconut milk and cooled melted chocolate with coconut oil.

Add in all of the other ingredients.

Stir through your HJ chopped chocolate last.

Bake for 30 minutes.

'Eggs' for Baking

Ingredients:

1 tbsp of chia seeds (either hole or freshly blended)

3 tbsp of water

Can't have eggs? Egg replacement in baking

How to make:

Soaked chia seeds for 5 – 10 minutes.

This will replace 1 egg in your recipe.

Flapjacks

Ingredients:

125g coconut oil

4 tbsp coconut nectar

1 cup coconut sugar

225g quinoa flakes

¼ tsp Himalayan sea salt

How to make:

Preheat oven to 150°C.

Mix all ingredients well and press into prepared tray.

Make sure your Flapjacks are about 1 inch thick.

Bake for 30 minutes.

Remove and stand for 5 minutes.

Please allow to fully cool before cutting and removing. They harden once cooled.

Once cooled, drizzle some HJ1 chocolate in the top and put in fridge to set. (optional)

Store in fridge.

S and J tips –
A quarter of the quinoa can be substituted with desiccated coconut.

Coconut oil can be reduced to 80g and 2 tbsp HJ peanut butter added.

Add dried fruits, nuts, seeds or HJ1 mini choc-chips.

Bake for a little longer to make them crunchier.

Fudge

Ingredients:

1/3 cup raw cacao powder

1/3 cup coconut oil (liquid)

1/4 cup coconut nectar

1 pinch of Himalayan sea salt

How to make:

Mix all ingredients together (blended is good for this).

Pour in a small container lined with baking paper.

Freeze for 2 hours or overnight.

Best stored in freezer.

Garlic Prawns

Ingredients:

500g prawns (green and already peeled)

¼ cup coconut oil

4 garlic cloves, finely chopped

¼ cup chives, thinly chopped

¼ cup of finely chopped parsley

1 tsp paprika

Salt and pepper to taste (we use about a ¼ tsp of each)

How to make:

In a bowl, mix together coconut oil, chives, garlic, parsley, paprika, salt and pepper.

Stir through your prawns.

In an already hot (medium - high) frypan, fry prawns until orange.

Serve on a fresh salad.

Ginger Ale

Ingredients:

2 cups water

One whole finely chopped Ginger

Coconut nectar

1 tbsp juice of a lemon

Sparkling water

How to make:

Combine water and ginger in a saucepan.

Bring to boil and let boil for 10 minutes.

Pour mixture into a jar with lid.

Add in ¼ cup coconut nectar and stir.

Place sealed jar in the fridge for 8 hours or overnight.

Strain the ginger pieces out with a nut bag so you are just left with liquid.

Add lemon and stir.

Add 2 tbsp of ginger mix to 1 cup of sparkling water.

S and J tip – You can add more ginger mix to your cup if you love it strong and if you want it sweeter, you can add a little stevia to your cup (the dried up leaf, not the chemical infused commercial crap).

Herb and Garlic Bread

Ingredients:

¼ cup flax meal

¼ cup coconut flour

1 tbsp baking powder

½ tsp Himalayan sea salt

¼ cup water

4 eggs

1 tsp coconut nectar (optional)

1 tbsp chopped fresh rosemary

1 clove of garlic, finely chopped

1 tbsp fresh herb mix

Cold pressed olive oil for drizzling when ready

How to make:

Preheat the oven to 180°C.

Mix all of your ingredients together.

Let sit for 1 - 2 minutes, allowing the coconut flour to soak up the liquid.

Shape your bread into ½ inch thick circles on a baking tray lined with baking paper.

Sprinkle your rosemary on top.

Bake for 20 - 30 minutes.

Once out of oven, drizzle with a little olive oil.

Eat warm.

Jam

How to make:

Blend chia seeds into a fine powder.

Add strawberries and coconut nectar and blend with 'chia flour'.

Pour in a jar and store in fridge overnight to allow to thicken to a jam consistency.

S and J tips -
If you have a sweet tooth, you can add extra coconut nectar.

You don't need to blend chia seeds.

You can use any berries (not just strawberries) if you like. Mixed fresh berries or even figs are yummy.

Ingredients:

2 punnets of berries (strawberries, blueberries etc) - about 3 cups

4 tbsp of coconut nectar

4 tbsp of chia seeds

Jam Doughnuts

Ingredients:

¼ cup of warm water

2 tsp yeast

1 tbsp of coconut sugar

½ cup of coconut flour

¾ cup tapioca starch

1 tsp guar gum

2 tbsp baking powder

2 tsp amaranth flour

½ tsp Himalayan sea salt

1 cup of coconut sugar

5 tbsp coconut oil

3 large eggs

Coconut oil (for frying Doughnuts)

Jam for filling (see our recipe on page 64)

How to make:

Preheat oven to 180°C

Mix the warm water, yeast and tbsp of sugar and let sit.
In a blender, mix the rest of your doughnut ingredients.
Pour in the yeast mixture and blend on high for 1 - 2 minutes until it thickens.
Let the mix sit for 1 - 2 minutes while it gets thicker and stickier.

Put the dough onto your bench dusted with a little Tapioca Starch so it doesn't stick.
Roll or pat out the dough to be 1 ½ inches thick.
Using a biscuit cutter or a cup, cut into 8 circles. (Dust the biscuit cutter with starch.)
Place the doughnuts onto a baking tray lined with baking paper.
Wipe each doughnut with a little water and cover with baking paper.
Cover the tray with a towel.

Turn the oven off, and place the covered tray into the oven.
Leave the doughnuts in the warm oven for 30 minutes to rise.

Slowly heat a layer of coconut oil in a pan.
Fry your doughnuts (If you heat it too high your Doughnuts will not cook fully on the inside.)
Turn the Doughnuts so they cook evenly.
Allow to cool on a wire rack.

Dig a hole inside the Doughnut to make room for filling.
Place jam into a piping bag or sandwich bag with a corner snipped off.
Poke the tip of the piping bag into doughnut and squeeze jam into the doughnut

S and J tip – You can blend some coconut sugar to make a powder and roll each doughnut in it!!

Jelly

Ingredients:

2 cups of freshly squeezed juice

Gelatin (check the label of how much to use it's normally around 2 tbsp)

Coconut nectar (optional)

How to make:

Take ½ cup of your juice and put in a saucepan and heat on low/medium heat.

When the juice is hot ,you can add your gelatin by pouring in slowly and stir continuously until the gelatin is fully dissolved.

Remove from the stove and let sit for a minute.

Pour the rest of your juice in your warm mixture.

Add 1 - 2 tbsp of coconut nectar if you want it sweeter.

Pour mixture into some jelly moulds.

Put Jelly mix into the fridge for a few hours or overnight.

S and J tip – Gelatin is really good for you if you get the right brand. Make sure it is grass fed beef.

Lemon Slice

Ingredients:

Crust
½ cup finely ground raw sunflower seeds
⅔ cup coconut flour
1 tbsp baking soda
2 tbsp coconut oil
2 tbsp coconut nectar
2 eggs
1 tsp pure vanilla extract
1½ tsp fresh lemon juice (about ½ a lemon)

Filling
3 large eggs plus 1 yolk, lightly beaten
½ cup coconut nectar
¾ cup fresh lemon juice (about 4 lemons)
3 tbsp coconut flour, sifted
1 tsp lemon zest, finely grated

How to make:

Preheat oven to 180°C.

Mix all of the crust ingredients together.

Lay baking paper in a baking tin.

Press the mix into the bottom of the baking tin.

Bake for 10 minutes.

Let cool while you prepare the filling.

Mix together all of the filling ingredients.

Allow the coconut flour to absorb for 5 minutes.

Pour the filling on top of the baked crust, and bake again for 15 minutes at 180°C.

Cool on a wire rack for 20 minutes.

Once fully cooled, remove from baking tray, cut into squares and serve.

Store in fridge.

Lollies

Ingredients:

1 cup freshly squeezed juice of choice

1 tbsp lemon juice

1 tbsp coconut nectar

Gelatin (read the packet for how much)

How to make:

In a medium saucepan, bring juice to a boil.

Allow to cool for 3 minutes, then stir in lemon juice and coconut nectar.

Very gradually, stir in gelatin (so it doesn't go lumpy).

Allow mixture to cool to room temperature.

Pour your lolly mixture into your shape moulds of choice.

Refrigerate for at least 3 hours (overnight is great).

Store lollies in fridge.

S and J tips -

Make sure you strain all of the 'bits' out of your juice after juicing.

If you want your lollies sweeter, add more nectar.

If you want them chewier, add a little more gelatin.

Use a good quality grass fed beef gelatin.

Marshmallows

Ingredients:

1 cup water (split into half cups)

Grass fed gelatin (read packet for how much)

1 cup coconut nectar

1 tsp vanilla extract

¼ tsp Himalayan sea salt

1 tbsp tapioca starch (for rolling marshmallows)

How to make:

In your blender/mixer, add the gelatin with ½ cup of water and let it sit.

Pour the other ½ cup of water in a saucepan along with the coconut nectar, vanilla and the salt.

On medium/high heat, bring the mixture to boil (about 8 minutes).

Immediately remove the saucepan from the heat.

Turn your blender/mixer to low/med.

Slowly pour the hot mixture in with the gelatin.

Turn the mixer to high and continue mixing for about 10 minutes until it becomes thick.

Line a baking tin with baking paper and sprinkle some tapioca.

Pour your marshmallow mixture into your baking tin.

Smooth the top and sprinkle a little more tapioca.

Let set for about 4 hours and then pull out of dish and cut.

S and J tips –
Instead of tapioca you can coat with desiccated coconut.

To make it tubular shaped, just cut it with a cookie cutter.

Meat Pie

Ingredients:

Filling
300g lean steak, cut into 3cm cubes
300g beef minced
2 tbsp tapioca starch
1 onion, diced
1 medium carrot, diced
1 cup chopped mushrooms
1 ¼ cups beef stock (see our recipe on page 12)
2 tbsp finely chopped fresh curly parsley
½ tsp Himalayan sea salt
Freshly cracked black pepper

Pastry
2 tsp whole psyllium husks
⅛ tsp guar gum
⅓ cup of warm water
1 ¾ cup of golden linseeds blended (flaxmeal)
½ cup tapioca starch
¼ tsp Himalayan sea salt
½ tbsp baking powder
1 clove garlic finely chopped (optional for more flavour)
1 tbsp paprika powder (optional for more flavour)
May need extra water

How to make:

Filling:
Place steak and mince in bowl and toss through tapioca.
Fry until browned.
Add onion, carrots and mushroom, stirring for 2 minutes.
Add stock, parsley, salt and pepper.
Let simmer over medium - high heat while you prep your pastry (20 - 30 minutes)

Pastry:
Preheat oven to 180°C.
In a small cup or bowl, combine the psyllium, guar gum and ⅓ cup of water. Mix and set aside for a few minutes so that it can thicken.
Mix the flaxmeal, tapioca, salt and baking powder in a blender.
Add the psyllium mix and blend on high.
If your dough is crumbly, add a little bit more water (1 tsp at a time) until it start to hold together.
Place you mixture between two sheets of baking paper and roll out very thin. Too thick and it will end up way too hard.

Spread your dough out in a pie tray (Family tray or minis) and add your filling.
Put a pastry lid on each pie (or one big ol' one on that family pie).
Bake for 25 minutes on 180°C.

S and J tip – Feel free to add whatever spices and seasoning to your pastry a you like to add different flavour. This pastry has a very strong flavour, so keep really thin (thinner than the photo) so it doesn't overpower the filling.

Milk (dairy free)

Ingredients:

Coconut Milk
1 baby coconut (white)
1 pitted date (optional)
1 cup of water (optional)

Almond Milk
100g of raw almonds (soaked overnight)
1L of filtered water
1 pitted date (optional)

How to make:

Blend all ingredients in high speed blender for 2 minutes.

Pour and strain through a nut bag into a glass container.

Coconut Milk:

Open baby coconut.

Pour coconut water into blender.

Scrape coconut flesh into blender.

Add date.

Blend for 2 minutes.

Pour and strain through a nut bag into a glass container.

Mini Pizza

Ingredients:

4 chicken breasts (skinless)

350ml Jar tomato paste (no salt)

All of your toppings. You can get to creative with this. (see our picture for ideas)

If you want cheese (to keep it dairy free) you can use goats feta, goats cream cheese or buffalo mozzarella.

How to make:

Preheat oven to 180°C.

Slice each chicken breast in half long ways and then those long pieces in half so you have mini pizza bases. (You can use round metal biscuit cutters if you want them perfectly round and use left over chicken for another meal).

The thinner you make your chicken slices the better.

Lay each cut chicken piece on an oven tray lined with aluminum foil.

Spread tomato paste on each base.

Add the toppings you want to each pizza. (We love to make a variety.)

Bake in the oven for 30 minutes.

Serve.

S and J tip -
The thinner you make your chicken slices, the better (if you know how to fillet fish, you'll be able to make fantastic pizzas)!

Ingredients:

Chips
4 sweet potatoes (1 per person)

Mince
1 large onion diced
1 large red capsicum diced
Mince (beef, chicken or turkey)
1 tin of organic whole tomatoes – nothing added (or cook your own and remove skin)
4 tbsp 'no salt' tomato paste
2 garlic cloves finely chopped
Pinch of Himalayan sea salt
Pinch of pepper
1 tbsp paprika
1 tbsp thyme chopped finely
1 tbsp basil finely chopped
1 tbsp coriander finely chopped
½ cup of chicken stock (optional, see our recipe on page 28)

Topping
1 roma tomato diced
2 avocados blended
Goats cheese or coconut yogurt (optional as a dollop on top to serve)

Nachos

How to make:

Preheat oven on 200°C.

Thinly slice 1 large sweet potato, leaving the skin on.

Lay out the slices on a large baking tray.

Sprinkle with Himalayan sea salt, paprika, and drizzle of coconut oil.

Cook until crispy, remove and set aside.

Fry onion, capsicum and mince.

Once mince is brown, add in your tin of organic whole tomatoes, tomato paste, garlic, salt, pepper, paprika, thyme, basil, coriander and stock. Simmer on medium heat for 10 minutes.

To serve, put sweet potato chips on bottom, then your mince and dollop of avocado with some tomato and the goats cheese or coconut yogurt on top.

Oreos

Ingredients:

Biscuits
1 ¼ cups tapioca starch
¾ cup quinoa flour
½ cup buckwheat flour
¾ cup raw cacao powder
1 cup coconut sugar
½ tbsp baking soda
5 tbsp coconut oil
1 egg
2 tsp vanilla extract
5 tbsp water
¼ tsp Himalayan sea salt

Oreo Filling
3 tbsp coconut butter
½ cup coconut oil
1 tsp vanilla extract
2 cup coconut sugar (blended
to a powder)

How to make:

Preheat oven to 180°C.

Add all of your ingredients to a bowl or high power blender and mix together.

Between two pieces of baking paper, roll out the biscuit dough to a nice even thickness.

This dough will not rise in the oven.

Using a small round biscuit cutter, cut your round shapes and put each on a oven tray lined with baking paper.

Make some patterns on the biscuit if you feel like it.

Bake for 12 minutes and remove from oven.

Allow them to cool on the baking paper and go hard before filling.

How to make the Filling:
Blend all ingredients together and spoon onto each biscuit.

Pesto Pasta

Ingredients:

½ cup – 1 cup of pesto (see HealthyJUNK1)

2 zucchinis put through a spiral machine (see HealthyJUNK1)

¼ cup of coconut milk or coconut cream

Squeeze of lemon or lime

How to make:

Cook pasta in a fry pan with a little water and 1 tsp of lemon or lime juice for about 1 - 2 minutes just until warm. It doesn't take long at all.

Take off stove and stir though pesto and coconut milk/cream.

It's ready to serve!!

S and J tip – Roast some extra pepitas and sunflower seeds to give it that extra crunchy goodness.

Pikelets

Ingredients:

½ cup coconut flour

½ cup tapioca starch

¼ cup coconut oil

2 tbsp baking powder

1 tsp pure vanilla extract

¼ cup coconut nectar

1 cup coconut milk

5 eggs

How to make:

Mix all of your ingredients together.

Add a little coconut oil onto pan to create a non - stick surface.

Pour mixture into hot pan to the size you want.

Flip Pikelets when you can see bubbles appear through them.

Cook other side until golden brown.

Chocolate pikelets:
For chocolate pikelets add one tbsp of cacao powder to ingredients before cooking.

S and J tip - Mixing in some HJ1 Chocolate (chips) is delicious too!!

Popsicles

Ingredients:

1 large fresh pineapple, cut into chunks

Juice of 1 lime

1 ½ cups full fat coconut milk

How to make:

Place pineapple and lime juice in a high power blender.

Blend until smooth and frothy.

Blend in the coconut milk.

Pour mixture into Popsicle moulds and freeze until hard.

S and J tip – Choose any fruit combo you like!! Get creative!

Prawn Cutlets

Ingredients:

¼ cup coconut flour

¼ cup desiccated coconut

1 large egg

20 green prawns (peeled, but with tail still attached)

3 tbsp coconut oil

How to make:

Mix your desiccated coconut and flour in a bowl.

Beat egg in a separate bowl.

Roll each uncooked prawn in the egg, then in the coconut mixture.

Put on a plate to take to stove top.

In a frypan, pour in a little coconut oil and allow to heat up.

Fry prawn cutlets on both sides until golden brown.

Serve with a side of green salad.

Raisin Bread

Ingredients:

½ cup banana flour

⅓ cup coconut flour

4 eggs

¼ cup coconut oil

¼ cup coocnut nectar

1 tbsp baking paper

1 pinch Himalayan sea salt

2 tbsp ground cinnamon

1 cup raisins

1 cup water

How to make:

Preheat the oven to 180°C.

Mix all ingredients (except raisins).

Stir through all of your raisins only at the end.

Add your mixture to a small bread loaf tin lined with baking paper.

Fill your tin to the top (this bad boy won't be rising much).

Sprinkle the top with raisins.

Bake for 45 - 60 minutes, depending on how moist you like it inside.

Please poke with a knife (or a thin metal cake tester) to test whether your bread is cooked through. If your knife comes out clean, it is ready. If not, your bread may need a little longer in the oven.

Let the bread cool before removing.

S and J tip – If you don't have a nut allergy you can use almond flour instead of sunflower seed flour and but you will need to add 1 tbsp of baking powder. May also need less time in the oven so check at about 70 mins.

Sausage Rolls

Ingredients:

Pastry
2 tsp whole psyllium husks
$1/8$ tsp guar gum
$1/3$ cup of warm water
1 $3/4$ cup of golden linseeds blended (flaxmeal)
$1/2$ cup tapioca starch
$1/4$ tsp Himalayan sea salt
$1/2$ tbsp baking powder
1 clove garlic finely chopped
(optional for more flavour)
1 tbsp paprika powder
(optional for more flavour)
May need extra water.

Filling
500g raw organic pork, beef or chicken
1 onion, diced
2 cloves garlic finely chopped
Freshly ground black pepper
Fresh Herbs of choice finely chopped
1 tsp Himalayan sea salt
1 egg

How to make:

Pastry:
Preheat oven to 180°C.

In a small cup or bowl, combine the psyllium, guar gum and $1/3$ cup of water. Mix and set aside for a few minutes so that it can thicken.

Mix the flaxmeal, tapioca, salt and baking powder in a blender.

Add the psyllium mix and blend on high.

If your dough is crumbly, add a little bit more water (1 tsp at a time) until it starts to hold together.

Place you mixture between two sheets of baking paper and roll out very thin (Too thick and it will end up way too hard).

Filling:
Combine meat and spices.

Beat egg in small bowl with fork.

Add half of the beaten egg to meat.

Put your meat into centre of your pastry in a long line.

Roll it up.

Seal the dough with remainder of beaten egg using pastry brush.

Cook for around 25 minutes, depending on how you like your meat.

Serve with HealthyJUNK1 tomato sauce.

Sorbet (raw icecream)

Ingredients:

2 frozen bananas

1 cup of frozen berries of choice (or frozen mango)

Egg white from 1 egg (optional)

How to make:

Blend frozen fruit for 1 - 2 minutes until smooth.

Add egg white and blend for 30 seconds to 1 minute to make more fluffy.

Strawberry Cupcakes

Ingredients:

Cupcakes
1/2 cup banana flour
1/2 cup coconut flour
1 tbsp baking powder
1 pinch of Himalayan sea salt
1/4 cup coconut nectar
1/4 cup coconut oil
4 large eggs
1 tsp vanilla extract
1 cup finely chopped strawberries

Icing
2 egg whites, room temperature
1/3 cup coconut nectar
1/4 tsp juice of a lemon
1 1/2 tbsp blended strawberries

How to make:

Cupcakes:
Preheat the oven to 180°C.

Mix all ingredients in a blender or in a bowl.

Spoon mixture in to cupcake cups.

Bake for 30 - 45 minutes.

Let the cupcakes cool before icing.

Icing:
Boil your coconut nectar in a saucepan for 1 minute.

Beat the egg whites and lemon juice until frothy.

While still mixing, slowly pour in the boiling coconut nectar.

Continue beating for 5 minutes, until the icing is cool to touch.

Stir in your blended strawberries SLOWLY (so the icing doesn't go runny).

Add a spoon of icing to each cupcake.

S and J tip – An electric mixer is great for the icing.

Sushi

Ingredients:

Rice
½ cup mixed quinoa (or blended cauliflower)
1 ½ cups water
4 nori sheets
2 tbsp apple cider vinegar (optional: use cauliflower rice from HealthyJUNK1)

Filling
½ small cucumber, washed and cut into batons
½ an avocado, peeled and thinly sliced lengthways
Creamed goat cheese
Freshly cooked chicken cut into thin strips
Grated tamari, to serve (optional)
Finely sliced ginger, to serve (optional)
Coconut aminos (optional for dipping)

How to make:

Place quinoa and water in a pot and bring to boil.

Simmer for 10 minutes until quinoa is cooked (it will fluff up to triple its original size and appear to have little 'tails').

Remove from heat and set aside to cool for 10 minutes.

Stir in the apple cider vinegar.

Lay the first nori sheet on a cutting board or a sushi rolling mat.

Spread a 1 cm thick layer of 'rice' evenly over the sheet, leaving a 2 cm strip along the top end (to allow for sealing).

Lay your fillings of choice (make sure it's not too much).

Moisten the 2 cm strip at the top with a pastry brush dipped in water.

Pick up the bottom edge of the sheet and carefully roll it tightly (away from you).

Repeat with remaining sheets.

Serve with tamari, ginger and coconut aminos (instead of soy sauce).

You can also serve with wasabi sauce if you like a good kick up the sinuses.

Sweet and Sour Chicken

Ingredients:

⅓ cup coconut Aminos
1 tbsp coconut oil
2 tbsp coconut nectar
½ tsp Himalayan sea salt
2 cloves garlic, finely chopped
1 tsp fresh ginger, grated
¼ tsp chopped mild chilli
4 boneless, skinless chicken
breasts chopped into 1-inch
cubes
1 red capsicum, diced
1 onion, diced
½ fresh pineapple, cut into
1-inch cubes (nearly 2 cups)
½ cup fresh spring onion
chopped
1 ½ cups soaked quinoa
(if you can, soak quinoa
overnight)

How to make:

Cook Quinoa in water until soft (this doesn't take as long as rice).

In a small bowl, whisk together coconut aminos, coconut nectar, garlic, ginger, chilli and salt.

Place chicken in a large pan and fry until brown with coconut oil and onion.

If you have lots of excess liquid, drain it.

Pour over coconut amino mixture and allow to heat with chicken.

Add capsicum, pineapple and spring onion.

Let simmer for 3 - 5 minutes.

Serve immediately with your cooked quinoa.

S and J tip – If you have any pineapple juice left over from fresh pineapple you can stir through while simmering.

For fun, serve in half pineapples as bowls.

Use pork instead of chicken if you want.

Sweet Scrolls

Ingredients:

Scrolls
¾ cup of coconut flour
½ cup amaranth flour
⅓ cup tapioca starch
½ tsp Himalayan sea salt
1 tsp guar gum
2 tbsp baking powder
½ cup of coconut sugar
½ cup coconut oil
2 large eggs
4 tbsp coconut nectar

Glaze (optional)
½ cup finely blended coconut sugar
1 tbsp water

How to make:

Preheat oven to 180°C.

Line a baking tray with a piece of baking paper.

Mix all ingredients together (blender is the fastest).

Roll out dough into long garden hose thickness pieces.

And then roll into the shape of a scroll bun.

Place the scrolls on your baking sheet and bake for 20 minutes.

When cooked, brush scrolls with the glaze while still warm.

Serve warm or cold!

S and J tips -

Best eaten that day.

If your dough sticks to the counter, just sprinkle some tapioca starch on it.

Tacos

Ingredients:

Cos Lettuce (for taco shells)

Chicken or Beef (or your choice of meat)

Avocado (either blended or chopped)

Grated carrots

Grated beetroot

Diced tomatoes

Diced mushrooms

Goat's Cream cheese or goats feta

Clove of garlic

Ginger (your choice how much)

Chilli (optional)

How to make:

Chop a clove of garlic, some ginger and mild chilli.

Cook in a pan with diced chicken or beef.

Rinse and lay lettuce sheets out on a plate to use as taco shell.

You can put all the fillings in separate bowls on the table for everyone to make their own.

OR

Add your desired filling to each lettuce leave (taco shell) and put on a plate and serve.

Yummy, and no painful taco shells embedding themselves into your gums!

Tartare Sauce

Ingredients:

1 cup of mayonnaise (see HealthyJUNK1)

1 tbsp coconut vinegar

1 tsp lemon juice

1 tsp ground mustard

1 tbsp finely chopped fresh dill

1 tbsp finely chopped flat leave parsley

Pinch of Himalayan sea salt (to taste)

Pinch of black pepper (to taste)

How to make:

Whisk together all ingredients in a bowl (stir through dill and parsley last).

Tortilla

Ingredients:

1 large cauliflower

2 eggs

¼ cup lime

¼ cup Cilantro

½ tsp of salt and pepper

How to make:

1 large cauliflower blended and cooked till soft.

Liquid squeezed out of it with cloth.

In a bowl, add eggs, cooked cauliflower, cilantro, lime, salt and pepper.

Mix and shape into round tortillas.

Put in a tray and lined with baking paper.

In oven for 375 for 15 - 20 minutes.

Get out of the oven and put in a fry pan for 1 minute both sides.

Enjoy!

Wicked Wings

Ingredients:

1 kg chicken wings
coconut oil (for cooking)

Wet mixture
¼ cup of natural hot sauce
(get a good quality, organic
additive free one)
½ cup coconut oil
1 tbsp tapioca starch
½ cup coconut milk

Dry mixture
1 cup tapioca starch
1 cup Sunflower seed flour
(just sunflower seeded
blended)
1 tsp black pepper
½ tsp Himalayan sea salt
1 tsp garlic
1 tbsp paprika

How to make:

Preheat oven to 200°C.

Heat and stir wet ingredients until they thicken on the stovetop in a saucepan (about 5 minutes).

In another bowl, combine dry ingredients.

Smother chicken wings in wet mixture and then dry mixture.

Place all chicken wings on a baking tray that is lined with aluminium foil.

Drizzle chicken with a little coconut oil.

Put in oven for 30 minutes (chicken will be golden brown and cooked through)

S and J tip – Choose your hot sauce depending on your preference for spiciness

Talk to us!

We'd love to hear from you, please let us know if and how this book has helped you; or tell us your family's story of going from junk food family to healthy family. Just shoot us a quick email at

sharnyandjulius@sharnyandjulius.com

Thankyou for taking the time to read our book!

Sharny and Julius Kieser

You can also follow us on social media by searching:
sharnyandjulius
The Kiesers

Lightning Source UK Ltd.
Milton Keynes UK
UKHW051123200720
366775UK00002B/2